"For a [...]
who listens [...]
opens her heart with love!

SPT
2019

Oh So Silly

Oh So Silly

Zany Tales from an Unconventional Mind

Sharon Trout, Ed.D.

Sharon Trout
sharontrout@ymail.com

Nandina Books
PO Box 251301
Little Rock, AR 72225

ISBN 978-1-7337964-0-8

Book and cover design: H. K. Stewart

Printed in the United States of America

This book is printed on archival-quality paper that
meets requirements of the American National
Standard for Information Sciences, Permanence of
Paper, Printed Library Materials, ANSI Z39.48-1984.

Dedicated to
KAY KILBURY

Contents

Happiness
is so much better
than depression.

Acknowledgements

Special thanks go to my sister Nancy Settle for proofreading my early stories and for believing that there was a book in me and encouraging me to write it.

I also want to thank Joan Neikirk and Carolyn Minga for typing and editing many of the stories and for sending them by email to me numerous times.

And special thanks to my publisher, H. K. Stewart, for his calm patience and sense of humor as he guided me through the process of putting a book together. I couldn't have done it without him.

I will always be indebted to Tina Coffin, who serves as a guide in the "Tell Your Own Story" class at *Life Quest,* a program for seniors at the Second Presbyterian Church in Little Rock Arkansas. She told me that I had a talent for writing stories and that I should pursue it. She planted the first idea that I could write a book.

Remembering Kay Kilbury

The first year I met Kay, I was working on my clinical rotations for my psychologist license at the Arkansas State Hospital and the Child Study Center. I was an older divorced mother of two college students, and the only way I could pay my bills was to live on $30 per month for gas and food. I had clothes from my previous job. An elderly friend had given me yarn, and I was knitting my daughter's sweater for her Christmas gift. I chose to do duplicate stitch on the front, being a new knitter and not knowing how difficult it was for a beginner. I was there on Christmas Eve, and it came time for the knit shop to close and I wasn't finished and Kay knew I couldn't finish it without help.

She sent the other girls home and said she'd stay on a few minutes and assured them she'd be all right. Six o'clock came and I was frazzled. Kay calmly said, "Stop worrying! We're going to finish that sweater if it takes all night." So, I relaxed and got it done before 7 p.m.

A customer of Kay's came in and brought Kay a chocolate cake that was still warm. I was picking up two abused children, David and Mary, from the Child Study Center to spend Christmas at my house. I had put my name on the gift tree at my church and had plenty of staple food, but Kay in all her generosity thought the children might enjoy chocolate cake. She said she already had plenty of sweets at home and why didn't I take the cake to David and Mary. I did, and they had cake for breakfast on Christmas morn. My daughter only recently passed the sweater on. Both children still talk about that Christmas being the best they ever had. And Kay was a big part in making it happen.

As the years passed, I grew to love Kay, including her gruffness at times. Her memory was phenomenal. She was able to remember what each customer of the Yarn Mart, her shop, knitted out of what pattern, and what yarn, and what changes were made. I knitted an off-white sweater with cables up the front, and black trim across the top of the front and back, and around the sleeves. I thought the sweater looked like something Audrey Hepburn or Jackie Kennedy might wear, and Kay agreed, to my delight.

I took the sweater to the cleaners and was horribly upset when they told me that it had gotten caught in the machinery. When I saw the sweater, it had one torn sleeve, and horrible, greasy black stuff was over most of the rest of the sweater. The lady told me to get an estimate of what it had cost and what it would cost to replace it.

Off to Kay I went. She remembered the type of yarn even though it was no longer available, how many skeins the pattern had required, how much the buttons had cost, and how many hours it would take for someone to knit it to replace it. I then presented the estimate to the cleaners with Kay's signature. The cleaners reimbursed me every penny—well over $300. And that had been quite a number of years ago.

And then Kay showed what a dear friend she was. I bought the yarn and the buttons, and as I was paying for them, she said, "Just leave that here with me. I'm going to knit that sweater for you. Let's take some measurements so it will fit right."

And that's how I came to be one of the few people who has a sweater knitted by Kay Kilbury, long-time owner of the Yarn Mart. I keep the sweater in the freezer so that moths can't get to it. Kay is gone now, but I have not forgotten her. I keep her picture in my memory box and my love of her kindness in my heart.

Wringing a Chicken's Neck

When I was young, I always wanted to do what the big people were doing. I wanted to sit at the big table with the grownups and not at the little table with the children. I thought I was as big as the grownups. And I was given as many responsibilities in my dysfunctional family as grownups had in other families. If the mousetrap caught a mouse during the night, it was my job to take the trap with the dead mouse somewhere away from the house to release it. I was the third child in the family, but for some reason, the duty fell to me.

Another duty that fell to me was pulling loose teeth. If a tooth of any of my three sisters was loose and on the brink of falling out, my mother would tell me to get the pliers and pull that tooth. From the time I was a little child not yet going to school, I would go get the pliers and pull any loose teeth that any of my sisters had. I was steady and quick, and no one questioned the practice at all.

We lived in the city for a while, and we had chickens and rabbits for food to eat. One day, Mother was going out to the chicken pen to wring a chicken's neck. I asked her to let me do it. She told me that I could, so I went out to the chicken yard and picked out a big white chicken. I had to chase her a while before I caught her, but I finally did. I grabbed both legs in one of my hands and started slinging her in circles with my right hand. I slung and slung her. But her head never flew off, so I switched to my left hand when my right arm gave out. So I slung the chicken some more. This is the way I thought Mother had done it. But the chicken's head would not come off for me.

Well, Mother got tired of waiting for me to come inside with the beheaded chicken, so she came to check on how things were going. Her first words were, "What are you doing?"

I replied, "I'm trying to wring this chicken's neck." Then she told me to put that chicken down and that was not the way to wring a chicken's neck. She said something about how she wouldn't want to eat that chicken that evening anyway the way it was staggering around. If I asked to try again, she would say something about my needing to get a little older. I never did learn how to wring a chicken's neck.

The Colquitt Girls
Hang a Painting

It was going to be a calm day—or so I thought. I was at my sister Nancy's house. Just by being there I should have known it would be anything but calm. When the two of us get together, it's anything but calm.

When I arrived, Nancy was standing on a two-seater couch holding a rather large painting in her hands as if she were going to hang it above the small couch. She had two nails in her mouth and therefore couldn't speak.

I'm not an expert decorator, but I do know a thing or two about balancing a room. I couldn't understand why she was hanging the larger painting over the small couch and the smaller painting over the large couch.

I joined her on the small couch. As I stood there beside her trying to assist her in the painting hanging, she noticed that I kept looking over my shoulder at the small painting hanging over the three-seater couch. She started looking at me every time I looked at the small painting hanging over the three-seater couch that was adjacent to the smaller couch.

She couldn't really say anything because she had both her hands on the large painting and two nails in her mouth. She just muttered, "Um thunk them bug painting sud go uver thr, cunt u?" And I replied with a monologue about how many seats each couch had and how the size of each painting would balance the room. (By this time Nancy had this, "Why does she have to be right?" look on her face and set the painting on the back of the small couch.)

"Here," I said, "let me take those nails out of your mouth so you can talk." I reached carefully for the nails and took them, and Nancy's whole body gave a little jerk— almost as if without the nails she were no longer able to maintain her balance. "Don't fall," I said. But I was too late. Her 5'11" frame was slowly going backwards. I felt her hand jerking on a thin gold chain that I was wearing around my neck. And then I saw her size 13 white tennis shoes sticking up from a rocking chair, and she was smiling. I asked her later why she was smiling. She said, "When I felt the rocking chair beneath me, I knew I wasn't going to hit the floor."

She got up, and it was then I noticed that my gold chain and cross were missing. I told her it was a $300 chain. I was really teasing her with a straight face. My son tells me, "Mother, when you do that, be sure to smile at the end so people will know you are teasing." This is a time I forgot to smile.

I also forgot to mention that my cousin Kay and her daughter Bethany and Bethany's son Ethan were coming over that day. Really, I'm not sure Nancy mentioned it to me. But I digress.

I noticed my chain was missing, and I asked Nancy for a flashlight so I could search for the chain. She got a flashlight for me and explained that it needed new batteries. I don't think Nancy believes in having extra anything around. She would rather have empty drawers than have drawers with extra batteries. When I turned the flashlight on, a thin ray of light was all that it could produce.

Well, there I was on my hands and knees with a weak ray of light pushing Nancy's new carpet from side to side, sneezing from my allergy, and finding nothing when the doorbell rang. In came my cousin Kay and her daughter and her grandson. Kay took one look at me and said, "See, Ethan, I told you it would be fun! Aunt Sharon is already on her hands and knees playing a game of some kind."

Nancy said, "No, she's looking for a $300 gold chain."

So I stood up and said to Nancy, "No, I was teasing about that, I just forgot to smile."

"You sure did," said Nancy. She has the same rule my son Jim does.

Ethan wanted to know what I was looking for, and I described the chain and cross. He listened attentively and then reached out his hand to a scarf I was wearing and held up a gold chain with a cross on it and asked, "Like this one?" He was holding the missing chain and cross. It had been hanging on my scarf all along.

So, I said, "Yes, that's it." And then we all ate and started comparing cell phones, but that's another silly story and too long to tell today.

One Hung Low

I did a lot of studying and training in Memphis, Tennessee, to be a psychologist. At that time the school was called Memphis State University. Now it's called the University of Memphis. I lived in West Helena, Arkansas, and the mental health center in Helena actually sent me to school to be a psychologist because it was hard to get a psychologist to come to Helena and also hard to keep one. So the mental health center worked out a deal with me where I would repay them by working two days for each day I had used educational leave to get my doctorate. I drove the 80 or so miles from Helena to Memphis twice a week to complete my studies. And one of the areas I studied was family therapy.

When I was doing training, my friend Jane and I would go to lunch. She got time to go to lunch, and I got a break from seeing people with Ray Gentry, Sr., a wonderful instructor. He ran the Family Life Enrichment Center and I was an intern there. Sometimes he would go to lunch with us. Jane and I loved to go to a Chinese restaurant. It had a difficult name that Jane has still not learned today (2019). But we called it One Hung Low. Ray would say, "Where are you girls going to lunch?" And we would say, "We're going to One Hung Low. Do you want to come with us?" And he would say, "No, I don't think so."

I called Jane and told her that I was going to include this in my book, *Oh So Silly*. I asked her if she could tell me the real name of that restaurant. She said, "No, it's still here today, and everybody just calls it One Hung Low." So, if you're ever in Memphis and you want good Oriental food, just stop somebody and ask them where you can find One Hung Low!

My Own Kind of Understanding

I graduated from St. Joseph's High School in Conway, Arkansas. There were 33 students in my class. We were a bright, energetic, creative group. We were the first class to have cheerleaders, and also the first class to have a yearbook. We even restored a senior class trip. We had barrels of fun. We still get together every two months to celebrate birthdays. We have remained good friends during the years. In October 2015, we celebrated our 50th high school reunion.

A member of our class had passed away, and a large group of class members went to another member's house for lunch after the funeral. When we were almost finished with the meal, one of the female members said that we needed to start thinking about our 70th. My mind was still on the 50th reunion. But everyone in the class had just turned 70 or would turn 70 that year. The female class member was thinking about the big 70th birthday party for all of us.

So, me with my reunion thinking was figuring that the 70th reunion wouldn't take place for 20 more years. I said, "Don't you think we ought to wait and see who is still around first?" Now Judi, my best friend, knows how I think, but she was sitting at a table too far away to tell me. It wasn't until I visited her that I found out that it was all about our 70th birthday and not about the 70th reunion.

Another thing learned slowly.

On Being Economical

Sometimes I have a brilliant idea, but then there are the others.

I bought a 10-pound bag of rice in one of my economical moves. I put it on a lower shelf and promptly forgot about it. After awhile, I started seeing flying bugs in the kitchen area and finally traced the source back to the bag of rice. I decided that I had to get rid of it since it was contaminated, and the fastest way to do this was to put it down the garbage disposal. I didn't know that raw rice would swell when combined with water. But it sure did.

When my husband came home, I had finished with all 10 pounds, but the sink was stopped up. He tried using a plunger, but that did nothing. It was early summer, and he was hot natured, and it seemed as though the house suddenly got hotter.

And then the questions started. "Whatever possessed you to put the rice down the garbage disposal anyway?" I explained that I thought it would grind up the bugs at the same time as I got rid of the rice. There were more questions with more unacceptable responses, but all of this verbal activity didn't unclog the drain. So then my husband got down to problem solving. He called Rote-O-Rooter, and they came that very afternoon.

They had to use what they called a "snake," and they just kept putting it in the drain. But that didn't work. After awhile, they started pulling it out, and then they said they were going to have to go get the industrial snake—that the one they had wasn't working. When they returned with the longer snake, they said it would reach all the way to the street. It did work, and my husband paid the bill. I never asked him how much it was.

After that, you would have thought I would try to keep a low profile. I tried, I guess, but that's not how it worked out. I was working at the Marianna clinic, and when we went to lunch, I saw a guy on the side of the road selling peaches. They were ripe and ready for eating or freezing. So I bought two bushels' worth. When my husband came home from work, I was in the kitchen busily peeling peaches. He looked around and then asked, "Where are you going to put all of those peaches?" I told him I was going to freeze them. And again he said, "Where?"

Finally I thought and realized that the peaches wouldn't all fit in the small compartment above the refrigerator and said, "Oh." So he went to town and bought a freezer and had it delivered that afternoon. We had them put it in a small room attached to the house that we called the "step down." Economically, it probably would have made more sense to throw the peaches away or give them away. But they sure did make good peach ice cream that winter and spring.

Things Learned Slowly, Part I

It only took nine years for me to realize I could chew gum on the right side of my mouth since the left side of my mouth had residual damage from my stroke in 2009. I would drool when I chewed gum on the left side. In 2018, I finally realized that if I chewed it on the right side, I didn't drool.

Blue Paper Shorts

I went to see the orthopedic surgeon to see if I had a torn meniscus. In forgetting that I might have to pull my pants up over my knees, I had worn slim, black leggings. When I got to the doctor's office, the nurse had me change into a pair of wide blue paper shorts. The doctor came in and examined my knee and explained it was some type of bursitis and that I needed extensive physical therapy.

This doctor liked to hear jokes and I like to tell jokes, so we spent some time doing that. And then he said, "You're good to go," and left the office. I had brought a short black raincoat and a purse and some other items, so I tried to collect everything, having left some items in the past. The black leggings that I had worn were actually hanging across the back of a black chair, so I did not notice them.

I left the examining room, and the nurse told me that I did not need to make a return appointment and that she hoped I would continue to make good progress in physical therapy. I thanked her for being so nice. I told her I'd see her the next time. And she said, "Ms. Trout, are you going to leave like that?"

"Well, I guess so," I said. Then she looked down, and I looked down to see what she was looking at. It's then that I saw the roomy blue paper shorts. I said, "At 69 years old, I could leave in these shorts and nobody would notice. But I like the black leggings that are in that room, so I'm going to go back and change."

The nurses just smiled when I came out and told them goodbye.

Blueberries

A friend of mine was coming over to pick up a five-gallon bucket of compost that I no longer needed. It was going to be a little while before he would arrive and I was feeling light headed, so I ate a small bowl of blueberries and lay down on my bed to rest. When he rang the doorbell, I got up and went to the garage to meet him and show him where the plastic bucket of compost was. We visited and talked about nothing in particular, but he ended up staying quite a while.

When he left, I put the garage door down and went back into the house and went to use the restroom. As I walked by my mirror, I turned to check myself, and I noticed that I had blueberry colored lips and teeth and that part of the blueberries were hanging from my teeth. All the time I had been talking to my friend, my mouth had looked like this and my friend had said not one word about the condition of my teeth. They looked horrible. I never said anything about it to him, and he never said anything about it to me, either.

Don't Hide Your Phone in Your Panties

It seemed like an ordinary Saturday—but with me, things are never as they seem. My two cats were making one-and-a-half-inch mountains in the carpet runner in the living room so they could hide behind them and take turns attacking each other. The cats had done this so frequently and had also run between my legs so often that it had become dangerous and I was forced to have someone adopt them. The lady who came to check on my life line had told me that if I was looking for someone to take my cats, she wanted me to call her first. I didn't know that her cat had recently died and that her two young girls wanted a cat. So I called her, and we agreed that she would call me when she was ready to come over and pick up the cats.

As I was waiting for the call, I realized I didn't know where I'd put my phone. My friends Bev and Steve were coming to pick me up to go to dinner, and I didn't know where my phone was. I had looked for it in all the usual places but hadn't found it anywhere.

I got my iPad out. It had "Find My Phone" on it. I pushed that icon, and immediately the circles appeared. They led me to my trash bin sitting on my driveway. I wondered—did I drop my phone by the trash bin when I carried out the trash from the house? Could I have dropped my cell phone by the trash bin and someone from my neighborhood saw it and picked it up?

I looked at my iPad, and it was showing 900 feet instead of 90 feet the way it had earlier. I went back through the house, and the numbers on the iPad started going lower. I was getting closer to my iPhone.

Then I went back through the house, and the numbers went lower again. They led me to a neighbor's house two doors down from my house. I planned to ask them if they had seen my phone—kinda like, "Did you steal my phone?" but in a nice way. I knocked and rang the doorbell, but nobody answered. (I have a host of angels who watch over me, and they were really working hard that day.)

I looked at my iPad, and suddenly the numbers were much higher again. So back to my house I went with the numbers going lower all the way back. I ended up in my bedroom closet with really low numbers that looked good, but I couldn't get them to go any lower because of the back wall in my closet. I went outside to the other side of the wall (into the living room), and then the numbers were high again.

It was time for Bev and Steve to come to get me so we could go to dinner. I went outside and sat on a small bench to wait for them to arrive. I decided that I would get Steve to help me find my phone because he's good at that sort of thing.

So there I was waiting for Bev and Steve to arrive, and suddenly my left breast begins to ring. Then I remembered—I put my cell phone in my bra. It was the lady who wanted the cats. She needed to reschedule to another day. I told her how glad I was that she was the one who called, because I was going to ask Steve to use "Find My Phone," and now he wouldn't have to find my phone in my bra. We laughed and scheduled another day for her to come and get the cats.

Bev and Steve arrived, and on the way to the restaurant, I told them what happened. We had dinner with our friend Paulette and laughed and talked. As we were getting ready to leave, Steve said, "Sharon, tell Paulette what you told Bev and me."

I told Paulette about losing the phone and finding it. Paulette laughed. And then she said, "You can't go with me to San Antonio with a group I'm going with."

"Why," I asked.

"Because right now I'm the most out-rageous, and if you go, I'll lose my standing."

As Steve was letting me out at my house, he said, "Sharon, just one thing."

I said, "What is that, Steve?"

"Don't ever hide your cell phone in your panties."

Giving Directions

I am a helpful citizen when it comes to seeing things that need to be reported to the police. One morning I was driving to a city that required me to get on the interstate. Not long before this, I had had a mini stroke, and my short-term memory was practically gone. I would have to think and think before I could say what I wanted to say.

As I was driving down the interstate, I saw a mattress on the side of the road, but part of it was lying on the interstate. I called 911 and told the officer who answered about the mattress. That officer said, "I need to connect you with the state police."

So very shortly I heard, "This is officer So-and-so of the Arkansas State Police. Can you tell me the nature of your call?" I repeated about the mattress. Then the state policeman said, "Give me the location of the mattress."

I explained that I didn't know the number of the interstate. I drive from Shoney's to Radio Shack. I know no numbers, no north or south. I just get there by landmarks. The officer then asked, "What interstate are you on?"

I said, "Well, if you were leaving Little Rock to go to Texarkana and you were on the interstate, right before you take the exit to Cracker Barrel, the mattress is on the right side of the road."

And thankfully, the state policeman said, "I know exactly where that is. I'll send someone out to pick it up right away, and thank you for calling."

I came out of that smelling like a rose!

Brown Church Balls

One Sunday afternoon, I attended a concert by a wonderful brass band. It was held in a church, and since my attention span is short, I started looking at the construction of the church. Large, dark brown massive supports were topped with wooden balls. I started counting the balls, but I had to start over because I couldn't remember if a ball had been counted or was supposed to be counted. I counted ball one and ball two, but when I got to ball three, the ball suddenly moved. That's when I saw it was the bald head of a black man. The color of his head matched the color of the wooden supports.

How to Sanitize Most Anything

Somehow I learned that if you want to rid a sponge of germs, the thing to do is to wet it and put it in the microwave for one minute—and remember to use tongs to remove it.

After I learned this way to sanitize things, I began to put more and more things in the microwave for one minute. I felt sure that all the things I handled this way were germ free.

I use a Water Pic, and I decided that since I had been sick I should sterilize the Water Pic attachment so I wouldn't be infecting myself from the attachment. I had been using the Water Pic attachment that was brushy.

The buzzer on the microwave dinged and I opened the door. There on the glass tray lay the Water Pic attachment. It didn't look the same as when I put it in. What I saw was the attachment with only one piece of brush. All the other bristles were lying on the glass tray. It was kinda cute with just the one sprig left. It might have been cute but it was definitely not functional.

Things Learned Slowly, Part II

On a trip to San Antonio, my sister Nancy, my cousin Beverly, and I went to a Mexican restaurant. We had frozen margaritas, and a Mariachi band played for my sister. After we finished our meal, we took a bathroom break and got ready to leave. We had trouble finding the door. A waiter went by, and we asked him to help us find the door to get out. He said, "Turn around." We were standing in front of the door.

It Looked Like More Than It Was

One morning I was getting dressed for work at the prison. I got up at 4:30 a.m. and usually left the house by 5:30 a.m. to be at work by 6:30 a.m. I had gained some weight and wasn't sure if the dress I wanted to wear would fit me. But I got it on and got it zipped and it was entirely too tight. I tried to unzip it, but there was no way I could get my arms around to reach the zipper to unzip it and get out of the dress. I went next door and rang the doorbell. I knew my neighbor's husband got up early to go to work. The only thing I could think of was to ask him to unzip the first part of the dress, and then I could finish unzipping the rest. I took a towel and wrapped it around my shoulders and went next door.

Well, the husband answered the door, and I told him that I wished that he would unzip my dress so I could get it off so I could put something else on so I could go to work. I still had the towel wrapped around my shoulders, but he couldn't see the pull tab for the zipper with the towel wrapped around me so I took it off, and he started pulling on the zipper tab. The tab wouldn't go down, and he was tugging on it really hard when his wife started coming down the stairs.

Just as she was about half way down, the zipper started moving quickly, and what she saw was her husband unzipping the whole length of the zipper in this tight dress. We both looked up and said "Hi" to her, and she just looked at us, and I said, "He'll explain it to you," and I went home. We remain good friends today. I saw the wife recently at the library and made plans for me to visit her in her new home soon.

How to Outfox a Cheater

It was a calm day. My oldest sister had been in the hospital in Conway. She had incurable cancer and had been nonresponsive for a day and a half, and I had been driving from Little Rock to Conway more times than I remember. My younger sister had not returned to see her eye surgeon after a corneal transplant and had an eye appointment with him on Friday. She was having some sort of eye problem, so I drove her from Conway to Little Rock and back, and then we went to the hospital where my sister was still mostly unresponsive. Over several days, my sister with cancer responded to treatment for pneumonia and returned to the nursing home.

It was my day to rest, and I was watching a movie—a romance. The movie was almost over and my phone rang. A man with a Spanish-sounding voice said, "This is Windows 7. Do you have your computer on?"

I responded, "No."

He said, "Go to your computer and turn it on. Hurry! Illegals are using your computer license to run illegal activities even as we speak. Do you have your computer on? What do you see?"

I responded, "I see a big square that says to download Windows 10."

He says, "Oh no, you don't want that. X it out."

And then he led me through a series of orders of what to look at that would prove that, since I didn't renew my license, illegals were using my computer for illegal services. He could move my little arrow all over. And then I said that I wanted him to call the guy who works on my computer and explain who he is.

He said, "Ma'am, I am from Windows 7. He won't know anything about me or what I do."

And later I said, "I'm going to call the attorney general's office and see if you are legit." Then I hung up. That's when he shut my whole computer down. It was a black screen. Then he called me again, and he was nice. He said he was trying to help me, and for $199 I wouldn't have to have anyone work on my computer for five years. He explained that the contract would say 10 years, but it would only be for five. He said it was time for me to fill out a form.

Now by that time, I was very suspicious, but also scared. I knew he could take over control of my computer and could shut it down. I had been on the phone a long time. And I was already late for meeting a friend at Barnes & Noble to get a movie I had lent him.

And this crook was filling out the form on my monitor. He was typing in $199, and I could see that the next space was for my signature. I just put my phone down by my laptop and picked up my purse and left. I could hear him shouting, "Are you there? Are you there?"

I went to Barnes & Noble, got my movie, and talked with my friend. I mentioned the caller and what he had said, and my friend got in gear fast—things like, "You've got to call the card company, he could wipe you out. Where is your card?"

Luckily, it was in my purse in the car. I got it, and he called customer service, and I told the lady, and she closed the debit card right then. When I got home, I got on my iPad and no money was taken. The next day, I got a new card and the crook called me all day long. As soon as I would block a number, he would change his number by one on the last digit and use that number, and I would block it. And now I have to take my laptop in to have it wiped clean.

In looking back, I made obvious mistakes, but when I got my wits about me, I made some smart decisions. I did call the attorney general's office. They told me that since my computer was hacked, I will now be a popular target and that in Arkansas I can sign up at the attorney general's office to get alerts that they send out about new scams.

How to Measure a Door and Frustrate a Contractor

My plan was to enclose my patio with glass windows and wood below them for about three feet with a nice door of wood and glass. I intended to keep the glider but get rid of the tubular chairs and the round table that were in the middle of the existing patio. I hired a contractor who had done a really nice job of getting my last house ready for sale.

The first thing he asked me to do was to give him five days that I would mark off to be available for different workers to come by and take measurements so they could give an estimate for whatever they would be doing.

I stayed at home available the first day and nobody came to take a measurement of any kind. Before the second day I was to be available, I called the contractor four times and left messages asking if anyone would be coming the next day to take a measurement. I got no returned phone calls from the contractor. The next day I called the contractor again and left a message that I would not be home that day and from now on I needed 24-hour notice if I was to be available. The contractor called me back in three minutes. After talking just a little while, the contractor decided that from then on he would get a time from the workers who would be coming to take measurements and he would then call me to set up the time. That sounded better to me, but he has yet to call me for any times.

After several weeks of no action, I called to see how many estimates he had (knowing he had zero), and he asked me to measure an existing door that was to be replaced with a louvered door. He explained the process of how he would have to measure the door, and then asked me to do it and call him with the measurements.

So then the fun began. I asked him to call my cell phone. I explained I would let the call go to voice mail so he could repeat his instructions about how to measure the door. He wanted to know when I would be home, and I explained that I was at my sister's house in Conway and had no idea when I would be back home. He said, "Well, just call me when you have the measurements." I said that I would and hung up.

Now, I am an intelligent person. I have a doctorate and I was a licensed psychologist until I retired in March of 2012, but suddenly I was struck dumb. After weeks of no action, now the contractor was asking me to do his job. This was just not right. I decided that somehow, he was going to have to carry his own load.

This was going to be fun. When I got home about 8:00 in the evening, I got out a metal tape measure. It was the kind that had a little thing on the end to hook over the end of what you are trying to measure. I took the measurements and called the contractor back and told him I had the measurements. After he got a pen and paper, the really big fun started. He said, "OK, tell me what you've got."

I set him up. I said, "Well, you know—I did my best, but I never could draw a straight line."

He said, "Oh, that's OK. Just tell me what you've got."

I said, "Well, the width of the door is one and a quarter inches and one more little mark."

He said, "That mark is an eighth of an inch, so that's one and three-eighths inches, and that's the depth, not the width."

"Oh," I said, "I called it the width." And I thought—he's going to get every one of these measurements without any trouble.

I was wrong.

He then said, "Well, what are the other measurements?"

"Well, across the door it is 28 inches and one little mark."

"That's the width," he said.

I said, "Oh, I used the wrong word; I called it across; I measured across the door from the side at the back of the door to just above where the handle is. Is it okay to measure there?"

He says, "Yes, that's fine. Well what was the length?"

"Is that the one from top to bottom?"

"Yes," he says.

"Well, that one is a little confusing to me," I said.

"What was confusing," he asks, and then said, "I really need to get these measurements."

It's been weeks of no action and now it's important. And it really has nothing to do with the patio.

So, continuing on with the top-to-bottom measurements that I'd told him were confusing to me, I said, "From the top to the bottom…" ("The length," he interjects) "…it is 78 inches, plus the length of the metal tape measure."

"Well," he said, "what size is the tape measure?"

"I don't know. It goes all the way to the floor, and the measuring part is inside the metal part, and I don't know how long the metal part is."

He said that tape measures either come in two inches or three inches, and he asked if I could see anything on the measure.

I said, "I don't think so," and then I said, "Oh, yes! Here it is: it says 12 feet."

In frustration he says, "No, that's not it. I really need these measurements. I'm going to have to come and take the door down anyway when I get the louvered door, so I'll just measure it then and measure where the hinges go." He wouldn't dare ask me to measure for hinges.

"So, are we good?" I asked.

"Yes, we're good," he said. "Thanks!"

"Okay," I said, "I'll talk to you later."

Needless to say, I hired a new contractor.

Driving Miss Nancy

My sister Nancy was in an automobile accident about the same time that a van plowed into my pretty red Ford Escape. Nancy was a little jumpy after her accident, so when I was driving my car, she would frequently stomp the floor on her side as if she were putting on the brakes. Everytime she did that, she would also suck in air as if she were very frightened. She did this so often when I wasn't having any problems with my driving that finally I told her that from then on she could have only five "Oh, shits" per ride. Any more than that and she had to get out of my car. We regularly had trips of two or three "Oh shits." One day, I knew I could drive my car between a couple of barriers, and Nancy used up all five of her "Oh shits" as I successfully drove between the two obstacles.

Finally, I decided to let Nancy experience how I felt. So we were driving along, and I made sure that there were no other cars or obstacles around. All of a sudden, I crammed my foot into the imaginary brake and sucked in my breath loudly. Nancy was momentarily frightened and asked me what was the matter. I told her that nothing was wrong, that I had just done that so she could see what it felt like to me when she did the same thing. She did fuss at me, but she was so much better from then on when she rode with me. Sometimes she didn't even use up one "Oh shit."

Math Story

My math problems started in the first grade. First grade was in a two-room school house in Charleston, Arkansas. The nun sent me to the chalkboard to work a simple math problem—something like $2+2$. When I am faced with a math anything, my mind just turns black. So I was standing at the chalkboard seeing black, and I wet my pants. The floors were unfinished wood, so it made a wet stain.

The nun walked over and asked, "Sharon, did you wet your pants?"

I looked at her and told my first lie. "No."

She looked at me with eyes that said, "I know you're lying to me." So she went to the other school room and brought my older sister Karen over and told her to check my panties to see if they were wet. But Karen didn't know where to check.

She touched high up in the back where they were dry and turned to the nun and said, "Her panties are dry."

So then the nun's eyes said, "Two liars in one family." The nun told Karen to walk me home to get some dry panties.

On the way home, our uncle drove by and said, "What are you two girls doing out of school?"

Karen told him that the nun was sending me home to get dry panties, then she added, "I felt her panties, and they're dry. The nun lied."

Evening in Paris

I was born without a sense of smell, but I didn't realize it until I was in high school and the chemistry lab caught on fire. Everyone was leaving the building except me. Someone noticed that I was still sitting at my desk and said, "Come on, Sharon, the school is on fire."

I went to my doctor, and he tested my sense of smell. The only thing I reacted to was ammonia, but the doctor said I was just reacting to the caustic part of the ammonia and was not really smelling it.

Before all of this, though, when I was much younger and hadn't discovered I couldn't smell, I bought a bottle of Evening in Paris perfume. The bottle was a deep cobalt blue color. (I still love that color.)

I would put on some of that perfume and try to smell it, but I couldn't smell anything. So I would put on some more. I would think that I hadn't used enough perfume. Sometimes I would spray it on a third time, and then I'd come out of the bedroom and find Mother. She would say, "Sharon, you have on too much perfume. That's a strong perfume, and you should only use a little bit." But I would think she didn't know what she was talking about because I couldn't even smell anything.

I would wait for a little while, then I would go back to my bedroom and get out the Evening in Paris perfume bottle and start spraying myself again. Then I would go back out into the house where Mother was working, and she would say, "Sharon, I told you not to put on any more perfume, and you did. If you put on any more, I'm going to take it away from you. I mean it."

Since I couldn't smell myself, though, I thought Mother couldn't tell the difference. But she could. And she took the bottle away for the rest of the day. The next day, she gave it back to me, and we did the same thing all over again.

She was patient and I was persistent.

I recently saw an ad in The Vermont Country Store catalogue for Evening in Paris perfume. The ad said, "Known for three decades as 'the fragrance more women wear than any other in the world.'" And later, "We're proud to offer this intoxicating French Eau de Parfumerie in its original 1.6 oz. cobalt spray bottle." And I thought "Maybe I could smell it now." And then I heard Mother say, "Sharon, I'm going to take that bottle away from you."

Things Learned Slowly, Part III

I was flying back home after a trip to California to visit a cousin. I was on a non-stop flight. The flight attendant handed out headphones, and a movie, Blue Jasmine, started to play. I couldn't hear anything through the earphones, but I watched the movie anyway. When the plane landed, I said to the lady sitting next to me that it would have been a better flight if it hadn't been a silent movie. "Oh," she said. "There was a knob on the side to turn up the volume."

When Not to Blow a Whistle

I had two cats, litter mates. They were so tiny when I got them, but of course, they grew. I bought books about how to train your cat to use the toilet.

I made a clicker as the book suggested to try to reinforce good behavior, but I never got around to stretching something that held a small amount of litter across the hole of the toilet to teach them to use that as their litter box. I really think it would work, but I was not home all day, and I gave up on their training pretty quickly.

My next thought was that I would train them to come to me when I blew a whistle. My husband had left me a really good military whistle that he had used when he coached a girls' basketball team. Well, when I blew it, the cats ran in the opposite direction, so I gave up on that idea, too.

Then I had a thought. Most of the time when I have a thought, it means trouble. My thought this time was "I wonder how loud it would be if I went into the pantry and shut the door and blew this whistle as loud as I could." Now you see why it is dangerous for me to have one of those thoughts that come to me out of the blue. But when I have a thought like that, I act on it fairly quickly before I think about it very much. So I had the whistle in my hand. I went immediately into the pantry, shut the door, and blew on that whistle as loud as I could.

I forgot to mention that I was wearing hearing aids and I did not take them out of my ears. The sound was deafening! And with hearing aids, I got a reverberation of that sound that I really can't describe. I don't know if this is a topic for simply sillies or simply stupid, but that was the loudest sound I have ever heard. When I told my sister I had done this, she just put her hand on her forehead, shook her head, and said, "What are we going to do with you?"

Problems
Hearing Aids Cause

I have worn hearing aids since 2012. About a year ago now, I was at the Athletic Club walking on a treadmill, and the guy next to me was riding a stationary bicycle. He mentioned to me that a friend of his had gotten new hearing aids that had a button that could be pushed and it would tune out the background noise. I decided I would go to the office where I got my hearing aids and ask if I could upgrade mine to that kind of hearing aid.

At that time, I had had my hearing aids for more than two years. When I asked Mark, the doctor who changes the settings on my hearing aids in his computer, if I could get that kind of hearing aid, he looked at me and said, "But you do have that kind." I took off my hearing aid, and he showed me the button that I should push to make it do that. It worked beautifully.

One morning, I was having breakfast in a restaurant, and three people were standing all within one foot of each other talking at the top of their voices. So I reached up, pushed the button for each hearing aid, and knocked out the background noise. Later that day I noticed what might have been either a bruise or a spider bite on my left arm, so I went to Urgent Care to get it checked out. It was late in the day, and I was the only one in the waiting room but I couldn't hear the TV. There was a large sign by the TV that said, "Do not change the channel." It didn't say anything about the volume, though, so I asked the receptionist if the volume could be turned up. She said,

"There's a remote. I will give it to you as soon as I finish what I'm working on."

A thought hit me. I remembered I had turned my hearing aids down. I reached up, clicked each button, and restored the hearing aids to full volume. Miraculously, I was now able to hear the television. I told the receptionist, "You don't need to give me that remote. The problem was me. I had my hearing aids turned down."

I told my friend Jane. Once again, she said, "Why do these things happen to you?"

My Wedding Robe

When Bennie Trout came to Little Rock to meet me, he brought with him a framed 8x10 picture of himself, which he gave to me within the first hour he was in my home. When he left he gave me a dirty Marine Corps t-shirt and his credit card, and he told me to buy a pretty white dress.

During the next week, I went shopping and then called to tell him about what I had found. I told him I had bought the prettiest long apricot-colored bathrobe. He listened to me as I described the robe. I told him that it had pockets and a long zipper all the way up the front. And then he asked me if I had found a pretty white dress. I told him that I hadn't found one.

Later, we got married and were married for 11 years. It was only after he died that I realized he'd wanted me to get a pretty white dress so I could wear it when I married him. It took me a really long time to learn that.

I still have the pretty robe. It's as pretty today as when I bought it.

My Crotch Hurts

As a retired person, I decided to exercise. A young woman at the athletic club I joined was really motivated to get me to exercise. She sent me messages about when the next yoga class would start—I didn't go. Finally, her efforts paid off. I joined her for a spin class. At that time, my urinary incontinence was not controlled, and I wore a fairly thick sanitary napkin in case of an accident.

The spin class involved riding a bicycle with a seat that felt like it was metal and about half an inch wide at the front. My motivator told the instructor, who went someplace and brought back a nice padded seat cover that felt much better. The instructor told me that since this was my first time, I should start slowly and only do the things I could do.

We started slowly, and the seat started to hurt. Now remember that I have been in mental health where you call it what it is, and I've worked in prison where you report exactly what the inmate said, so my grasp of language terms is quite broad.

Well, the seat kept hurting me, and when the rest of the class stood up on their pedals and pedaled faster, my legs wouldn't lift me up, so I continued to sit and pedal in pain. After a while, the pain was too great. I got off my bike, and as I walked past the instructor, she asked if I was okay. I told her yes, but that my crotch hurt and I was going to walk.

As I walked out the spin class door, I saw the physical therapist I had been working with, and he said something about my legs getting too tired for the spin class. I told him the problem was that my crotch had started hurting. He smiled and explained that a better choice of words might be….

About that time, my motivating friend came up and asked me if I was okay, and I again explained about the painful crotch, and she told the physical therapist that I used unusual words sometimes because of the stroke and working in the prison. I turned to the physical therapist and asked him what the word was that he said was more socially correct, and until the time I stopped working with him, he never remembered the word.

Pork and Beans

My sister has been known to say that I have been outrageous since birth. I have been. Sometimes I am a little embarrassed by something that I have said or done.

When I was still in grade school, I happened to be eating lunch next to one of the smartest students in my class. To this day I do not know what possessed me to tell her that my family was very poor. I told her that we were so poor that we had pork and beans for dinner every day during the week. And that Mother took the little piece of bacon out before she served us. I told my classmate that

Mother used them on Saturdays when she put the collected pieces of bacon in water and cooked them to make soup for all of us.

In reality Mother cooked fried chicken and fish with hush puppies and all sorts of good food. She was an excellent cook. I'm so glad I never told her about this. When I think about this, I can hear her saying, "That's the craziest thing I ever heard." But she would have had a twinkle in her eyes, and she would be trying not to smile.

The Day I Felt Like a Man

I think most people know what urinary incontinence is, but just in case, it's a condition where you can't hold your pee. I have it, but now I have a pacemaker for my bladder that keeps me from wetting on myself. When this event took place, I did not have what they call an interstem, which is the pacemaker.

I was at work one day and I had an accident. Usually I kept a change of clothes in my car, but that day I didn't. I told the director of the program that I needed to go buy some new clothes to wear. She said, "Just go." She had already told me in the past that I was certifiable and she no longer wanted details. If I needed to take care of personal things, I was just to tell her that and no more.

So I drove to Dillard's looking for a pair of black Traveler's pants. Traveler's pants are made out of a stretchy fabric that doesn't wrinkle. When I got there, the only sales clerk was a lady who looked about 80 years old. I asked her to help me find a pair of short Traveler's pants in black. The only size that fit me came only in long, but I said I'd take them.

Next, I asked her where the panties were located. She took me to a different area. The frilly panties were all about $15 to $20 each. I wasn't willing to pay that, so I had another idea. I thought I'd buy a package of men's briefs, wear one pair, and then give all three of them to my son—an economical idea. I asked the elderly sales clerk to show me where the men's briefs were located. That got an unusual look from her, but she took me to another area of the store.

I wanted to get a package of the men's briefs that were like shorts—not boxers—but the kind that came down on your legs. The clerk helped me find them, but she did seem a little puzzled. I had a new sanitary pad in my purse so I was okay that way, and it had an adhesive backing. I asked the clerk if I could use the dressing room to change clothes, and with that puzzled look again, she said yes. This was after I had paid for the items. I asked her if she had any safety pins. She said all she had were a few paper clips. I told her I'd try that, and she gave me the four she had.

When I went into the dressing room, I soon realized that men's shorts had extra fabric for their "package" and that my sanitary napkin stuck to it but was hanging loose between my legs and the paper clips did not hold on the stretchy Traveler's fabric of the pants.

In psychology we have a phrase called "acting as if." It means you just assume a look and act as if everything is okay. It was afternoon when all of this happened, and I only had about two hours more to work. I assumed the "I am just fine. I am like I always am." I was working at the prison then as the psychologist. As I walked up to the locked gate, my long pants were flopping around my shoes and at times I was walking on parts of the pants. The sanitary napkin was swinging free between my legs, and I thought, "I bet this is how men feel."

Things Learned Slowly, Part IV

I was sitting in bed one day, and the bed started to vibrate softly. I thought that there was a feature on my bed that the salesman had forgotten to tell me about. I wasn't sure what I had done to activate that feature, so I began to look around for a switch of some kind that I had not noticed.

It was then that I saw my phone on the bed next to me, and it was lighting up from an incoming call. My bed was not vibrating. I had turned my phone to silence, and it was vibrating while it lay on the bed next to me.

So much for hidden features to my bed.

Sick Gums

It was Thanksgiving. I had the flu and had been in bed for several days. I also had a urinary track infection. And I was anemic. I had fever and had been too sick to take care of personal hygiene. I finally decided that it was time to brush my teeth. The dentist had given me a mouthwash that was supposed to help irritated gums.

So I stood by the bathroom sink and looked in my mouth to check the color of my gums. I was horrified to see that they were bleeding around every tooth in my mouth. I started to beat myself up for not using the mouthwash every day, and then I remembered I'd just eaten sugarfree popsicles that were red, and I realized my gums were not bleeding at all.

Oh so silly.

Why Do People Listen To Me?

One evening I was having dinner with a friend of mine and his sister and brother-in-law at a restaurant called Mimi's. The restaurant serves these very large muffins, and each of my friends got one with their meal. A muffin didn't come with whatever I had ordered. The waiter brought what I thought was a sauce for the muffins. I was thinking that the muffins were like bread pudding and were served with a whiskey sauce. So the three of them poured the sauce on their muffins and started to eat them.

One of the people asked if the sauce was supposed to be sweet, and I said yes it was. About that time, the waiter came back to the table, and I asked him if the sauce he had served with the muffins was supposed to be sweet. He got a funny look on his face, and then he told me that what he had brought out was salad dressing for our salads. I had thought that I was so smart to know about the whiskey sauce. They just laughed at me, and the waiter asked if they would like new muffins, but they had already eaten most of their muffins and didn't want new ones.

I just have a way of seeming to really know things, and people believe me. They really should question some of the things I say.

Why I Buy Jam

When I was newly married, I tried to be a cook, but I was born without a sense of smell and could only taste sweet, sour, bitter, and salty. I could taste no flavors and still can't. But that was not the only trouble. I also had attention deficit hyperactivity disorder, so my mind flipped from one thing to another. Today, that problem is somewhat controlled by medication. My husband said that he could always tell when I was cooking something because I would not be in the kitchen.

Well, one day I decided to make some kind of berry jam. I got the strainer out and started following the directions. It said to cook some kind of berry for a while, and then strain the juice. So I cooked the berries, put the strainer in the sink, put the berries in the strainer, and saw the juice run down the sink drain. The next direction said, "Take the strained juice and mix it with water." It was then that I realized that I should not have let the strained juice run down the sink.

Since I had no juice to make jam, I dumped the cooked berries down the garbage disposal, cleaned my mess, went to the store, and bought jam. That is the very last time I ever made jam.

We Had a Little Wreck

My dad had a horrible temper, really terrible. When he got mad, his brown eyes turned red.

One Christmas my older sister, Karen, came home from nurse's training, and she and I went to Kathy's birthday party. My mother had taken care of Kathy ever since she was two or three years old.

When we were driving back from the birthday party, Karen was driving the car that day. The car was a big Buick with chrome hanging all over it. It was light green and white. It was my car to drive, but Karen wanted to drive that day since it had been a long time since she had driven the car.

We came to an intersection with a stop sign, and a car was coming from the right, but Karen must not have seen it. She drove right through the intersection and hit the car, which ricocheted across the street and knocked down a small tree, and our Buick stopped with its front facing the back of the other car. The Buick's rear end was in the middle of the street. Its horn was blowing, and Karen's knee was bleeding. Her panty hose were around her ankles.

Very quickly the police car arrived with red lights flashing. Luckily, the officer working the wreck was a friend of my dad's. The wrecker also arrived with blue lights flashing. The fire engine arrived also with red lights. Water was spurting from the hydrant where our car had knocked it over.

The officer told me I needed to call my dad. He knew how my dad was and told me to try not to upset him. I called my dad. When he answered, I asked him to come pick up Karen and me.

He said, "Why don't you just drive home?" I told him that I couldn't because we'd had a little wreck. Then he wanted to know where the car was and said he would come to get us.

By the time my dad got there, the tow truck had our car hanging from a winch. The spewing water had stopped spewing, but the street was wet and the tree that was knocked over was dripping water. Blood had dried on Karen's knee and leg. My dad's friend was still there. He was waiting for my dad. He told Karen and me to stay back until he had talked to my dad.

Then my dad got out of his car and looked at the view. The officer walked up to my dad, who said, "A little wreck. I'd hate to see a big one."

He was so shocked that he didn't get angry. He and the officer made arrangements about

the car. As my dad drove us home, he didn't
ever say much about the accident. I think the
technique of telling him that it was a little
wreck and then shocking him with the reality
of it robbed him of his anger.

My Sister Nancy

Nancy is 14 months younger than I. She is kind, super nice, and so much more gullible. When we were about three and four years old, we went exploring in the asparagus patch. I knew what it was, but for some reason, Nancy did not. So when we were there in the asparagus patch, I had an idea. I decided to feed Nancy raw asparagus. Not the big mature stalks. I searched for the small shoots that were just sprouting from the ground. I would pick a short asparagus spear, brush it off, and say, "This is a good one, Nancy. Eat it." And Nancy would eat it. I have no idea how many

I fed her. At any rate, that evening at dinner (then we called it supper), Nancy wasn't hungry. Mother asked her what was wrong. Nancy said her tummy hurt so Mother didn't make her eat.

Later that evening, Nancy started to throw up a vile green liquid, and Mother asked her what she had been eating. Nancy said, "Those little green things that Sharon gave me to eat."

Mother looked at me. "Sharon, what did you feed Nancy?"

I said, "I fed her little asparagus. "But they were the new ones."

Mother said, "I know you knew better than that."

I hung my head as if I felt guilty. I really didn't, but Mother accepted it as sorrow. I felt relief at not being punished. I think Nancy would have fared better if Mother had punished me, because that very summer my cousin Beverly and I "cooked" gizzards in water in little pots set on rocks. When they were cooked (when we got tired of stirring them), we called Nancy to eat one, which she did. She didn't eat the whole thing. There we had cooked the gizzards for what seemed like hours and she spit it out in less than two minutes.

I wasn't always mean to Nancy. One day when she was about three years old, she climbed a tall ladder that Daddy had left leaning against the roof of our house. When Mother saw her sitting on the roof, she backed out of Nancy's sight. She called me over to her and told me that Nancy was sitting on the roof and that she was afraid if Nancy saw her, she might think she was in trouble and might get upset and jump down. So Mother told me to climb the ladder and tell Nancy to turn around and climb back down with me. And that's what I did. I told her to turn around and put her foot on the top rung and then the next foot and so on. We backed our way down the ladder, and when we got down, everybody acted as if nothing unusual had happened.

Nancy says sometimes I boss her. I think I need to remind her at those times that I saved her life.

I read this story to Nancy, and she said, "That's not the way I remember it. You dared me to climb the ladder and get up on the roof and said 'I'll be right behind you.' I climbed it and turned around and sat down, and you were still on the ground, shaking your head 'no,' and saying 'I'm not coming up there.' I started crying and I was frozen on the roof. Then you went and told Mother and Mother made you go up there and get me down. And I think that was punishment enough for you. You had to climb the tall ladder when you didn't want to."

But Nancy doesn't hold a grudge. Years later she went to become a Sister of Mercy, a nun, and she took the name Sister Sharon Mary. I asked her why she took that as her name, and she said, "Because I loved you so much."

A Mountain out of a Molehill

I live at Woodland Heights. It's a senior retirement and assisted-living place. I had lived there for eight months when the situation that I'm going to tell you about happened.

I was at breakfast one morning and happened to be sitting next to a lady I had teased and joked with before. This morning, I had shared with her some of the "things learned slowly" that I had written for the book I was writing.

As we talked, she mentioned that one of the residents who lived there with us had been diagnosed with prostate cancer and had had his prostate removed. My reaction was one of horror. I said, "Oh no, I am so sorry that he had to have that done." In my mind I was thinking "Why did they have to remove his penis? Couldn't they have done something less invasive?"

I said to my friend that it reminded me of Miss Bobbit, a woman who made the headlines in the past when she cut off her husband's penis. My friend looked shocked and said that it wasn't his penis. It was just his prostate. We got tickled then and laughed.

Things Learned Slowly, Part V

*O*ne day when I was taking a shower, I closed
my eyes so that I could wash my face, and everything went dark. My first thought was, "Oh, no.
They've turned off the electricity."

Funny Doctor

I felt bad and had been running a low grade fever every afternoon. I was on a powerful antibiotic but was just not getting any better, so I went to see my doctor, and he asked if I could take steroids. I told him that I could not because they made me manic and I ended up in the psych unit of a hospital. So he decided to give me an inhaler that had some steroid in it and told me to rinse my teeth after I used it to get rid of the steroid that might linger there.

Then he said, "And if it starts to make you act funnier than you normally do, you need to stop using it."

Good Honest People

In January 2010, I had saved $2,000 in cash to go on a cruise, but a friend of mine called from Colorado (where he had flown to be with his ill sister) to say that she wasn't expected to live many more days. I thought I needed to be with him to support him during his time of loss. I hurriedly bought a ticket on Southwest Airlines and flew to Denver where my friend and his nephew were to pick me up.

There was a layover in Dallas, and I went to the airline counter to check when the flight would take off. After a while, I started to go to a restaurant, and as I walked by the airline counter, a ticket agent named Tanya Ham asked to see my ticket. I set my purse on the floor and got several things out to find my ticket. One of the things I got out was the $2,000 in a bank envelope. When I repacked my purse, I didn't notice that I left the bank envelope on the floor and went on to the restaurant. A passenger, Nico Digioia, from another flight came by and picked it up and turned it in to the ticket agents. They contacted the bank on the band on the money and found out my name and locked the money in the safe for their airline.

In the meantime, I had ordered lunch, and when I started to pay for it, I couldn't find my money—it was just gone. I was sick about it. About that time, Tanya, the ticket agent, saw me in the restaurant and asked if I was missing anything. I told her I had lost $2,000, and she said, "Come with me." When I started walking with her, I started crying and shaking from relief. The agents sat me down on the side of a column where I was out of view of others. They asked me what they could do for me. I was in shock. I said all I wanted was some lotion for my hands. And one of the agents got some of her own lotion and gave it to me. The agents, besides Tanya Ham, were Judy Townsend, Mary Ann Rujas, and Cindy Ferguson.

Then Mr. Digioia came back, and I got to tell him "thank you" and explain that the money was to be used to visit a friend who was dying from cancer. He said he knew when he saw it that the owner of the money needed it more than he did.

Days later when I was on my flight home, I told this story just as I have written it here to a young man sitting next to me on the flight. He said, "Lady, you have just saved my life. I was going to end my life when I got home after I got off this plane. I could see no good in mankind. But you have restored my faith and given me a reason to live."

We talked further about him getting a counselor when he got home. He seemed to have a positive attitude when he left.

Later, I looked up Nico Digioia and sent him a reward. He split the money between his church and his wife's school soccer team.

And I get an email birthday card every year.

I Learned a New Language

I worked as a psychologist for about 15 years, and while doing that I saw and heard more things than you can imagine. I reassured a teen girl that I did not have a drill to bore a hole in her head to let her nature out where she could not have sex. Her brothers had convinced her of that. I explained to an intellectually-challenged male, also a teen, that I could not show him how to put a condom on but that he should ask his shop teacher instead, and no, he should not practice sex on the family dog.

Part of my job as a counselor in the Delta was to have group therapy in a school system that was entirely black. I learned a whole new set of words that the first through sixth graders called each other about the color of their skin—high yellow, chocolate, ashy…

Recently, I called a business to ask if a certain person was working. I knew that I was talking to the black lady who greeted me when I had been there before. She asked me to describe the worker I needed to talk with. I told her about how his hair kinda stood up on top. And then I told her that I did not mean to offend her in any way by what I was going to say because the worker had been really helpful, and she said she wouldn't be offended. So I told her his skin was high yellow. She told me she knew exactly who that was and did he have buck teeth? I said, "Yes," and she told me what time he would come to work.

When I told my own children about the conversation, they both said, "Mother, you didn't say that, did you?" The lady on the phone and I were fine. But not my children.

And then I went to work in the prison system—talk about a new set of words. My dad was a bricklayer, and I thought his language was bad. Mother used to tell him she would have to hire criers to come to his funeral. His language didn't compare to the set of words used in the prison system, though. I worked there for six years until I retired. Inmates talked about "in the real world" and "in prison," because the two worlds were that different.

Just One Drink of Alcohol a Day

My oldest sister couldn't say, "Papa" the way my mother did when she was talking to her father. She called him, Appa." We had an Appa Miesner, my mother's father, and an Appa Colquitt, my dad's father. I think my dad was an alcoholic, but he was never professionally diagnosed. I think his dad was also an alcoholic, but that was just my opinion. When Grandma Colquitt died, both she and Appa Colquitt were already in a nursing home. His doctor ordered him a shot of whiskey every day. He was given that by the nursing home staff. My dad brought Appa a fifth of whiskey and put it between his mattress and box spring. Appa never really limited his alcohol consumption.

I can still hear my mother saying, "Well, Grandma Colquitt can say there's never been a drop of alcohol in this house, but she sure can't say that about the barn. Milking cows doesn't give him those bleary eyes and make him stagger when he walks."

With that kind of heritage, I decided I would be an alcoholic if I ever drank. I was over 40 years old before I drank any alcohol. Then I drank a wine cooler at a friend's house. I didn't get drunk, and I didn't keep drinking after I finished one. I bought a four-pack and put them in the refrigerator.

One night I was driving home, and I started thinking about drinking one of the wine-coolers. I couldn't wait to get home—but when I got there, I found that my friend had polished off the last one. I was furious. Now, I had whiskey and wine in the house, but I didn't want that. I wanted a wine-cooler. I decided I was an alcoholic. I started going to AA meetings, and I told my children that I was an alcoholic. My son told me that I wasn't an alcoholic, but that if I wanted to belong to a group, that was probably a good group to join.

After a year, I got a one-year coin for staying away from alcohol. That had been easy for me. Now staying away from sugar—that was a different story. I chose to attend meetings where they had cookies or snacks. I gained weight but I never missed a meeting— 90 meetings in 90 days. I finally realized that I was not an alcoholic.

Back to Appa Colquitt. One night he and an orderly shared the fifth of whiskey that was hidden. The story I heard from my mother was that sometime during the wee hours of the morning, Appa and the orderly were making too much noise, and one of the nursing home workers went to investigate. What they found was Appa in a wheelchair and the orderly pushing it, and they were trying to pop a wheelie with the wheelchair.

I never heard if the orderly lost his job or not. I did hear that the nursing home administrator had a talk with Dad. From what I overheard, it seemed that the administrator informed my dad that if she ever found alcohol in any form in Appa's room, he would be discharged from the nursing home and he would never be readmitted. That was the only nursing home in that city, and my dad must have paid attention to the administrator because Appa was still a resident there when he passed away.

DENSA Founding Member

When my daughter was in the 10th grade, we were shopping one day, and when I saw a Merle Norman store, I said, "I need to go in here," and we both went inside.

I asked the lady at the counter if she had a lipstick brush that would keep the brush part out without a person having to push on the little metal part sticking out from the side.

She said, "Let me show you what we have." She brought out a gold-colored thing about five inches long. She said, "This is the only one we have. We just take the cap off and push it on from the bottom and it pushes the metal part in and that holds the brush out."

I said, "Oh, that's like the one I have at home."

As my daughter and I left the shop, she asked, "Mother, do you know what MENSA is?" I told her I knew it was an organization for intelligent people. She said she was going to start a new organization for me and she was going to call it DENSA.

From then on when I would do something silly, I would say, "That's one for DENSA," and then laugh about it.

I asked my daughter about the DENSA event recently and she said, "I don't even remember that, Mother."

The Duck House

Several houses back, I lived in a house that had a screened-in back porch. I would invite people over and grill hamburgers and corn on the cobb. There was a creek behind the backyard fence, and when it rained the water would rise up close to the fence. Some ducks lived farther down the creek close to a sort of spillway. I believed that near dark, the ducks would swim upstream and would swim behind the fence and quack.

One evening I was grilling dinner for some friends, and the ducks started quacking. I explained to my friends how the ducks swam upstream in the evening, and my friends started to laugh. They said, "That's a good one Sharon," as if I'd told a joke. When I told them that I wasn't teasing, they said they knew that it was frogs croaking. I asked them if they were sure, and they said that they were positive. I couldn't believe that I had been wrong all that time. But it did make sense. I had never heard of ducks swimming upstream to quack.

My Bed

Let me tell you about my bed. I sat on one that a friend of mine had, and it was wonderful. So when I moved earlier this year, I treated myself to an adjustable bed that was expensive, but I thought it would be wonderful like my friend's bed. No need to put pillows behind me to be at the perfect angle to watch TV.

The first problem was that I kept falling out of the bed. If I tried to sit on the edge, I kept sliding out and landing on a wooden floor. My bruises from this were numerous but not impressive. One set of sheets I tried to use were too slick. I really slid out of the bed when I put them on the bed.

I tried numerous measures to prevent my sliding falls. My son suggested that I put my walker next to the side of the bed. The depth of the walker meant that it had to be a short distance from the side of the bed. So when I slid out of the bed, I still landed on my behind and once again I had bruises.

A friend brought me a handicap device to use with the idea that it would prevent falls. That would have worked, but I didn't use it correctly. The device was like a short step stool with two chrome bars extending straight up on one side and no bars on the other. The bars were connected at the top by a third bar that had a place for me to hold on to it. The stool part was a little too high for the bed. I would step up on it and then jump down onto the mattress. It was absolutely useless when I tried to get out of bed because I didn't have enough strength in my arms to pull me up so that I could stand on the stepstool part. So I would scoot down the bed to get to a spot where I didn't have to use it. But then when I tried to get out of the bed, I would slide right out and onto the floor. One time I had a bag of popcorn that was freshly popped, and I didn't take it out of my right hand so that I could hold the handle on the top of the chrome uprights. I could have switched the popcorn to my left hand, but I thought that all I had to do was step up and then jump into the bed. Of course I didn't do that. I stepped up on the stool part and then I lost my balance. I fell backwards and the handicap device fell over the top of me. The bruises from that were truly impressive. I had someone take a picture so I could see what my hurting behind looked like. And I had my physical therapist spray Biofreeze on it just to get some relief from the pain.

Clearly something had to be done. I bought a box of adhesive backed Velcro. My idea was to put strips of Velcro all over the top of the bed's frame. I planned to put one side of the adhesive Velcro on the top of the frame and the other part of the Velcro I planned to stick to the mattress. So I called a friend of mine to come over and hold the mattress up while I was sticking the Velcro to both parts. He agreed to help me. He had previously gotten a sheet of plastic webbing the size of the bed in the hope that it would keep the mattress from sliding. We knew what the problem was. The mattress slid a little each time I got out of the bed. That resulted in the mattress hanging over without a frame underneath it. And when I tried to sit on the edge of the bed, the mattress had no frame to support it and it just went down and I would slide out of the bed. My last set of bruises put Rorschach ink blots to shame.

So while my friend was holding the mattress up on its end, he discovered the problem. I had been sleeping on the top of a firm cloth that should have been on top of the frame, not on top of the mattress. And the mattress was facing down and positioned next to the framing fabric. No wonder it was shifting. The mattress had nothing to be against since it was extending beyond the frame. In effect, it was just extending out above air. And when I sat on the edge, it just leaned downward and then I would slide down it and land on the floor. So my friend told me to forget the Velcro. We took the sheets off and flipped the mattress. It stopped shifting, and I stopped sliding down the edge and landing on the hardwood floor.

After that, my bruises went away and I began to get a good night's sleep. From then on the anxiety of falling out of bed disappeared. No more bruises on my behind.

About the Author

Sharon Trout, Ed.D, is a retired psychologist who makes her home in Little Rock, Arkansas. She has two adult children and three grandchildren.

Over the course of her career, she has had a wide variety of work experiences, including as a Head Start teacher, remedial reading teacher, third-grade teacher, mental health center therapist, one of three psychologists in Arkansas doing assessments and approvals for the Medicaid waiver program, and psychologist for the Arkansas Department of Correction.

She earned her bachelor's degree from Arkansas State Teachers College in Conway (now the University of Central Arkansas) with honors in English, as well as master's degrees in both early childhood education and counseling. She completed her doctorate in counseling at Memphis State University and became a licensed psychologist.

She started writing again after she retired and attended a class called "Write Your Own Story" in the Life Quest program for seniors at Second Presbyterian Church in Little Rock. The facilitator in that program, who told her she had a real talent that should be pursued, encouraged her to choose topics that came to her rather than to use the weekly ones suggested on the guide sheet. *Oh So Silly* is her first book.